Cindy Pawlcyn's
Appetizers

Cindy Pawlcyn's Appetizers

Photography by Laurie Smith and Ed Anderson

TEN SPEED PRESS
Berkeley | Toronto

Ten Speed Press
PO Box 7123
Berkeley, California 94707
www.tenspeed.com

Distributed in Australia by Simon and Schuster Australia, in Canada by Ten Speed Press Canada, in New
Zealand by Southern Publishers Group, in South Africa by Real Books, and in the United Kingdom and
Europe by Publishers Group UK.

Front cover photograph by Ed Anderson
Back cover photograph by Laurie Smith
Cover and text design by Toni Tajima
Production by Colleen Cain

Library of Congress Cataloging-in-Publication Data on file with publisher

Printed in China
First printing, 2009

1 2 3 4 5 6 7 8 9 10 — 13 12 11 10 09

Contents

Those Nuts

2 cups raw shelled pistachios, almonds, pecans, peanuts, or walnuts

$1/2$ cup confectioners' sugar

Peanut oil or vegetable oil, for deep-frying

Sea salt

Cayenne pepper

Blanch the nuts in boiling water for 2 minutes. Drain and toss immediately with the confectioners' sugar, mixing well to coat the nuts evenly.

Heat 1 to $1^1/_2$ inches oil to $375°F$ in a heavy straight-sided pot. Add the nuts in batches, and fry for 1 to 2 minutes, until crisp and golden brown.

Using a slotted spoon, transfer the nuts to a rack or fine-mesh screen to drain (don't use paper towels because the nuts will stick!). Allow the oil to come back to temperature between batches.

Sprinkle the nuts with salt and cayenne to taste while still hot. Now, see if you can keep from eating them all up before company comes. You can also use them as a salad or dessert garnish.

Chile-Garlic Peanuts

MAKES A BIG BOWLFUL

2 heads garlic

$1/4$ cup peanut oil or vegetable oil

2 pounds shelled raw peanuts, with skins (use red-skinned Spanish peanuts for an authentic Oaxacan bar snack)

2 to 4 fiery-hot dried chiles, such as chiles de arbol or pequín chiles, slightly crushed

1 tablespoon kosher salt or sea salt

Grated zest and juice of 1 lime

Separate the heads of garlic into cloves. Trim off the root ends, but don't peel the cloves. Put the oil in a pan large enough to hold everything (a wok or double-handled pan would work well), and heat it until almost rippling—you want the oil nice and hot. Add the garlic, peanuts, and chiles; cook, stirring and shaking continuously, for 10 to 12 minutes, until the peanuts have darkened. Add the salt and lime zest and juice to the pan and give it another good stir and shake.

Pour out into a serving bowl and watch them go!

Black Pepper Mini Biscuits

MAKES 12

2 cups flour

1 tablespoon baking powder

1 teaspoon kosher salt or sea salt

$^1/_2$ teaspoon freshly ground black pepper

$6^1/_2$ tablespoons unsalted butter, cut into small cubes

$^3/_4$ cup plus 1 tablespoon buttermilk

1 egg

Preheat the oven to 400°F. Grease a baking sheet and set it aside.

Combine the flour, baking powder, $^1/_2$ teaspoon of the salt, and the pepper in a food processor or a large bowl. Work in the butter until the mixture resembles coarse meal, using short bursts of the food processor, a stand mixer fitted with the paddle attachment, or a pastry blender if mixing by hand. Add the buttermilk and mix quickly, just until everything clumps together. Turn the dough out onto a smooth, lightly floured surface and finish it with a few pats of the hand. Roll the dough $^3/_4$ inch thick. Cut into $1^1/_2$ or 2-inch rounds with a pastry cutter, and place the biscuits on the baking sheet. Gently press the scraps together, being careful not to over-work the dough, and cut out more biscuits.

Whisk the egg and the remaining $^1/_2$ teaspoon of salt until frothy, and brush over the biscuits. Bake for 12 to 14 minutes, until golden. Cool on a wire rack. These are best used fresh but can be reheated by placing them in a 300°F oven for a few minutes.

Gougères

4 or 5 eggs

Kosher salt or sea salt

3/4 cup water

1/3 cup unsalted butter

3/4 cup flour

3/4 cup (3 ounces) finely grated highest-quality Gruyère cheese (real Swiss is best)

Preheat the oven to 375°F to 400°F. Line a baking sheet with parchment paper.

Beat 1 of the eggs with a pinch of salt and set it aside. Combine the water, butter, and 1/4 teaspoon salt in a saucepan and bring it to a boil. Reduce the heat, add the flour, and whisk until the batter comes away from the sides of the pan. Cook for 1 to 2 minutes longer. Transfer to the bowl of a stand mixer and beat in 3 of the eggs, 1 at a time, beating until smooth after each addition. Add the last egg only if the batter seems too thick. The dough should be like a thick cookie dough. Stir in the cheese, saving a little to sprinkle on the top before baking.

Pipe or spoon the batter onto the prepared baking sheet, about a teaspoon of batter for each. Brush with the beaten egg and sprinkle with the remaining cheese. Bake for 12 to 16 minutes, until golden and puffed. Serve them hot from the oven.

Whole Roasted Garlic with Croutons

SERVES 6

6 very large heads garlic

$^3/_4$ cup extra virgin olive oil

2 or 3 bay leaves, fresh if possible (use Turkish bay, never California bay)

3 or 4 sprigs thyme

$^1/_4$ teaspoon kosher salt or sea salt

Freshly ground black pepper

1 baguette

Olives, cherry tomatoes, and roasted peppers, for serving (optional)

Preheat the oven to 300°F. Cut a thin slice off the very top of each head of garlic to expose the tops of all the cloves. Set the garlic heads in a 9 to 10-inch-wide shallow baking dish. (For best results, use a terra-cotta dish that will hold the heads together snugly.) Pour the olive oil slowly over and into each head, distributing it as equally as possible. Scatter the bay leaves and thyme over the garlic, and season with the salt and pepper to taste. Cover the pan with aluminum foil and bake for 1 $^3/_4$ hours, until the garlic is very soft and tender. Don't rush it; older garlic may take longer. Drain and reserve the oil, and set the garlic aside. Discard the bay leaves and thyme.

To make the croutons, preheat the oven to 375°F. Cut the baguette at a severe angle. You need 12 to 18 slices, each about $^1/_4$ inch thick. Brush 1 side of the slices with the reserved oil from the garlic, and bake oil side down for 5 to 7 minutes, until crisp and golden. You can also grill the bread slices over coals.

If you've roasted your garlic ahead, reheat it either in a 375°F oven or on the grill (doing it on the grill adds a great smoky flavor). Put 2 or 3 crisp croutons and a head of garlic on each serving plate, and pass dishes of olives, cherry tomatoes, and peppers.

Crispy Sesame Crackers

MAKES 2 TO 3 DOZEN

1 1/2 teaspoons active dried yeast

1 teaspoon sugar

1/3 cup warm water

1/3 cup plus 1 teaspoon cold water

2 cups flour, or more as needed

1 tablespoon unsalted butter, cut up

2 teaspoons kosher salt or sea salt

1 egg

2 tablespoons sesame seeds, preferably a mix of black and white

Combine the yeast, sugar, and warm water in the bowl of a stand mixer fitted with the dough hook. Let rest for 8 to 10 minutes, until foamy. Add the 1/3 cup cold water, then add the flour, butter, and salt. Mix to combine on medium speed until smooth and elastic, pulling the dough down off the hook if necessary. If the dough is sticky, add a little more flour. Gather into a ball, place the dough in an oiled bowl, turn to coat lightly, cover, and set aside in a warm place to rise for 1 to 1 1/2 hours, until doubled in size.

Preheat the oven to 350°F.

The easiest way to make very thin crackers is to pass the dough through a pasta machine. Roll them out as thinly as possible into 6-inch-wide, 3- or 4-inch-long strips. The goal is for the crackers to be almost paper-thin. I have found that it helps to roll out strips of dough, let them rest for 5 or 6 minutes, and then roll them out again. I repeat again if necessary. Lay the strips of dough on a nonstick baking sheet or a baking sheet lined with parchment paper. Beat the egg and the 1 teaspoon cold water, and brush the crackers with the egg wash. Sprinkle with the sesame seeds, then score the strips of dough to make triangular shapes (they'll break apart into individual crackers when they bake).

Turning the crackers as necessary, bake for 7 to 10 minutes, until they are a deep gold. Transfer to a rack to cool, then store in an airtight container for up to 1 week (or less, if humidity is high).

Hard-Boiled Eggs with Best Ever Tapenade

SERVES 6

Tapenade

1¹/₂ cups best ever Empeltre olives or other black olives, pitted (avoid Kalamatas)

1¹/₂ teaspoons Dijon mustard

2 tablespoons extra virgin olive oil

¹/₄ teaspoon freshly ground black pepper

Grated zest of ¹/₂ orange

1¹/₂ teaspoons coarsely chopped garlic

3 pieces soft oil-packed sun-dried tomato, coarsely chopped

2¹/₂ teaspoons coarsely chopped fresh flat-leaf parsley leaves

2¹/₂ teaspoons capers, rinsed

9 eggs

2 teaspoons kosher salt or sea salt

For the tapenade, combine all the tapenade ingredients in a food processor and pulse until they reach the smoothness you prefer. I find it's more interesting in the mouth to have a few bigger pieces—they give the tapenade a nice bite. Refrigerate until needed.

To hard-boil eggs Cindy-style, put them in a pot with enough cold water to cover by 1 inch and add the salt. Bring to a boil, reduce to a simmer, and cook for exactly 7 minutes. This will give you yolks that are bright and a tiny bit soft. Peel the eggs under cold running water. Slice them in half and arrange them cut side up on a platter or an egg dish, if you have one. Put a spoonful or two of tapenade in the center of each half egg; serve while the eggs are still warm.

Tapenade keeps for a very long time. I've always used it up before it has gone bad. Keep it in a covered jar in the refrigerator, with a thin layer of oil over the surface to keep it from drying out.

Plantain Chips with Cindy's Backstreet Kitchen Mojo and Cilantro-Garlic Dip

SERVES 6

Dip

1 cup mayonnaise

1 1/2 teaspoons minced garlic

1/4 bunch cilantro

2 tablespoons capers

1/4 teaspoon sea salt

1/8 teaspoon freshly ground black pepper

Mojo

12 small cloves garlic

1/4 teaspoon sea salt

1/4 cup freshly squeezed bitter orange juice

1 1/2 teaspoons cumin seeds, toasted and ground

1/2 cup extra virgin olive oil

1/4 teaspoon freshly ground black pepper

3 unripe plantains

Sea salt

Oil, for deep-frying

2 limes, cut into wedges

For the dip, coarsely chop the leaves and tender stems of the cilantro. Rinse and mince the capers. Combine all the dip ingredients in a small bowl and mix well. Chill and reserve until needed.

For the mojo, put the garlic and sea salt in a blender and pulse until finely chopped. Add the orange juice and cumin, and process finely. (If you don't have bitter orange juice, use half sweet orange juice and half lemon juice.) With the blender running, slowly add the olive oil in a steady, thin stream, and continue processing until the mojo is emulsified. Season with the pepper.

Have a container of ice water ready for soaking the sliced plantains. Cut off the tips of the plantains and peel. You may need to make a few lengthwise slits along the ridges of the peel to loosen it first. Add a few shakes of salt to the water. Slice the plantains lengthwise about 1/16 to 1/8 inch thick (this is best done with a mandoline), and soak them in the ice water for 15 to 20 minutes. Drain the plantains. Heat 1 1/2 inches oil to 365°F in a heavy straight-sided pot. Carefully lower a few slices of plantain at a time into the oil, taking care not to over-crowd the pan. Fry for about 1 minute, until crisp, transfer to paper towels to drain, and salt while hot. Allow the oil to return to temperature before frying the next batch.

Serve the chips with separate ramekins of the dip and the mojo, and plenty of lime wedges for squeezing.

Mustards' Famous Onion Rings with House-Made Ketchup

SERVES 6

Ketchup

3 1/2 pounds tomatoes, peeled and chopped

1 to 1 1/4 pounds apples, peeled if using green ones, chopped

3 onions, chopped

1 1/2 cups sugar

2 cups high-quality cider vinegar

1 tablespoon sea salt

1/2 teaspoon cayenne pepper

6 black peppercorns

6 allspice berries

6 cloves

Peanut oil or vegetable oil, for deep-frying

3 cups flour

1 tablespoon kosher salt or sea salt

6 large yellow onions, very thinly sliced on a mandoline

3 tablespoons minced fresh chives or scallions

For the ketchup, combine all the ketchup ingredients in a large stainless steel pot and bring to a boil. Reduce to a simmer and cook, uncovered, for about 2 hours, until it is the consistency of commercial ketchup. Allow it to cool slightly, then puree in batches in a blender until very smooth. Return to the heat for several more minutes to thicken further, stirring often. Strain and cool.

Heat at least 3 inches oil to 375°F in a heavy straight-sided pot. Combine the flour and salt in a large stainless steel bowl and mix well. Now toss in a few slices of onion and separate the slices by hand into individual rings. Get all the rings coated with some of the flour-salt mixture and transfer them to a strainer. Shake with abandon over the bowl to remove excess flour.

Transfer some of the rings to the frying basket. It is very important not to overcrowd the pan, so start with just a few to get a feel for the process. Check the oil temperature to be sure it's at 375°F, then carefully lower the basket into the hot oil. With a light touch, keep the rings moving almost constantly, using tongs to lift, separate, and turn in the oil as they cook. Carefully remove the onion rings when they are golden brown and crisp. Shake the excess oil from the cooked onion rings and pile them up on a big plate. Repeat with the remaining onion rings, frying them in as many batches as necessary. Sprinkle with the chives, and serve immediately with some ketchup on the side.

Avocado-Papaya Salad

1 or 2 ripe papayas
(about 1 pound)

Papaya Seed Dressing

2 tablespoons papaya
seeds

3 tablespoons freshly
squeezed lime juice

3 tablespoons rice
vinegar

5 teaspoons honey

$2/3$ cup olive oil

2 small cloves garlic

$1/2$ teaspoon cumin
seeds, toasted and
ground

1 teaspoon sweet paprika

$1/4$ teaspoon sea salt

Pinch of freshly ground
black pepper

2 cups baby mâche

2 cups baby arugula

2 or 3 avocados, sliced

$1^1/_2$ tablespoons toasted
hazelnuts, coarsely
chopped

Freshly ground black
pepper

1 lime, cut into 6 wedges

Split the papayas in half lengthwise. Scoop out the seeds, and set aside 2 tablespoons of seeds for the dressing, picking off any membranes attached to the seeds. Peel the papayas and cut crosswise into $1/4$-inch-thick slices.

To make the dressing, combine all the dressing ingredients in a blender and blend until smooth.

To serve, dress the mâche and arugula with half the dressing, and pile this in the center of 6 salad plates. Alternate slices of papaya and avocado across the greens and drizzle with the remaining dressing. Sprinkle on the nuts and some freshly ground black pepper, and place lime wedges on the side. Or if you prefer, you could compose the plate with the fruit on the bottom and the greens on top. Either way, it's yummy.

Roasted Red Pepper, Tomato, and Feta Salad with Lemon Vinaigrette

SERVES 6

2 red bell peppers, roasted, peeled, and cut into 6 pieces each

3 vine-ripened tomatoes, cut into 6 pieces each

1/2 cup thinly sliced red spring onion or scallions

2 ounces feta cheese, cubed

1/4 teaspoon freshly ground black pepper

1/2 cup of 1 or 2 chopped fresh herbs, such as cilantro, basil, or mint

Vinaigrette

2 tablespoons balsamic or red wine vinegar

Peel of 1 preserved lemon, minced

Juice of 1 lemon

1 tablespoon Dijon mustard

1/4 teaspoon kosher salt or sea salt

1/4 teaspoon freshly ground black pepper

1/2 cup extra virgin olive oil

Toss the bell peppers, tomatoes, onion, and cheese in a large salad bowl. Add the pepper and herbs and mix thoroughly.

For the vinaigrette, in a small bowl, combine the vinegar, lemon peel, lemon juice, mustard, salt, and pepper, and mix well. Slowly whisk in the olive oil, stirring until emulsified.

Pour the vinaigrette over the salad, using just enough to coat—not drown—the vegetables. Divide among 6 plates and serve. Drizzle any remaining vinaigrette over individual plates, if desired. This salad is great served with roasted garlic and extra croutons (see page 17) or spiced flatbread (see page 35).

Honey Walnut-Stuffed Dates with Spicy Greens and Three Cheeses

SERVES 6

1 cup shelled walnuts

3 tablespoons honey

12 fresh Medjool dates

Vinaigrette

1 tablespoon balsamic vinegar

1 shallot, thinly sliced

Pinch of kosher salt or sea salt

Pinch of freshly ground black pepper

3 tablespoons extra virgin olive oil

2 cups loosely packed arugula, watercress, or other greens

5 to 6 ounces Cowgirl Creamery Mt. Tam triple-cream, Brie, or Saint André cheese

6 ounces Tomme de Savoie cheese

5 ounces fresh Chabis goat cheese

Preheat the oven to 350°F.

Toast the walnuts for 7 to 10 minutes. Remove from the oven, let cool, and then coarsely chop. Combine with the honey in a small bowl.

Halve the dates lengthwise, remove the pits, and stuff with the walnut mixture.

For the vinaigrette, in a small bowl, combine the vinegar, shallot, salt, and pepper, and mix well. Slowly whisk in the olive oil, stirring until emulsified.

Gently toss 2 tablespoons or so of the vinaigrette with the greens. Divide the greens among 6 plates, placing them in the center.

Cut each variety of cheese into 6 pieces. Place a piece of each kind of cheese and 4 date halves around the edge of every plate. Drizzle a few drops of the remaining vinaigrette over the goat cheese and serve.

Spiced Flatbread Salad with Tomato, Radish, and Cucumber

SERVES 12

1 pint cherry tomatoes

$^1/_2$ bunch radishes

1 (4-inch) piece cucumber

1 celery heart with leaves

4 ounces Spiced Flatbread (page 35) or Crispy Sesame Crackers (page 19)

Vinaigrette

2 tablespoons red wine vinegar

$^1/_4$ teaspoon minced garlic

$^1/_2$ teaspoon toasted ground cumin

$^1/_4$ teaspoon sea salt

$^1/_8$ teaspoon freshly ground black pepper

6 tablespoons olive oil

6 tablespoons Greek-style yogurt (optional)

$^1/_2$ cup chopped fresh flat-leaf parsley (optional)

1 teaspoon minced fresh oregano (optional)

Halve the tomatoes, slice the radishes, peel, seed, and dice the cucumber, and chop the celery. Break the flatbread into good-size pieces. Place the tomatoes, radishes, cucumber, celery heart, and flatbread pieces in a large bowl.

For the vinaigrette, in a small bowl, combine the vinegar, garlic, cumin, salt, and pepper, and mix well. Slowly whisk in the oil, stirring until emulsified. Pour over the flatbread mixture and toss thoroughly.

Divide the salad among 12 plates and add a drizzle of yogurt to each. Finish with a sprinkling of parsley and oregano.

Braised Mushrooms with Spiced Flatbread

SERVES 6

1 cup flour

1/2 cup masa harina

1/2 teaspoon cumin seeds, toasted and finely ground

1/2 teaspoon sea salt

1/2 teaspoon black peppercorns, ground

1/2 cup plus about 2 tablespoons water

Mushrooms

1 ounce dried porcinis

3 tablespoons olive oil

1 tablespoon butter

4 large portobellos, stemmed and cut into bite-size pieces

1 clove garlic, crushed

1/4 teaspoon sea salt

1/8 teaspoon freshly ground black pepper

1 tablespoon finely chopped fresh basil

Juice of 1/2 lemon

1/2 cup mascarpone

2 ounces finely shredded Parmesan

Combine the flour, masa harina, cumin seeds, salt, and pepper in a large bowl and mix well. Work in the water a little at a time, just until the dough comes together. Cover the bowl with plastic wrap and let the dough rest at room temperature for 30 minutes, or to hold it longer, refrigerate it.

Preheat the oven to 425°F. Place a perforated baking sheet or a baking stone in the oven. Lightly dust a work surface with flour. Divide the dough into 8 equal pieces and roll each into a paper-thin 7 to 8-inch round, stacking the finished rounds with parchment paper between. Bake for 1 1/2 to 2 minutes, until golden brown and crispy, turning several times.

Place the porcinis in a small bowl with very hot water to cover. Soak for 20 to 30 minutes, until soft. Scoop out and pat dry. Pour the water through a fine-mesh strainer and reserve.

Heat the olive oil and butter in a large sauté pan over medium-high heat, until frothy. Add the mushrooms, and sauté for several minutes, until they have begun to caramelize. Add the garlic and cook for 30 seconds, until aromatic. Add the mushroom soaking liquid, simmer for a minute or two to reduce, then add the salt, pepper, basil, and lemon juice and simmer until the mushrooms are glazed and nearly dry.

Just before serving, preheat the oven to 425°F. Smear the flatbreads with the mascarpone, sprinkle with the mushrooms and the Parmesan, and bake for 2 to 3 minutes.

End o' Summer Tomato Crostini

Vinaigrette

2 tablespoons red wine

2 tablespoons red wine vinegar

$^1/_2$ tablespoon honey

$^1/_8$ teaspoon sea salt

Pinch of black pepper

1 tablespoon Dijon mustard

$^3/_4$ cup extra virgin olive oil

2 pounds really tasty vine-ripened tomatoes

1 sweet onion

1 tablespoon chopped fresh oregano, plus more for garnish

2 tablespoons extra virgin olive oil

$^1/_2$ tablespoon sea salt

$^1/_4$ to $^1/_3$ teaspoon freshly ground black pepper

Rustic country bread

1 cup arugula

1 tablespoon minced fresh chives

$^1/_2$ cup sharp, flavorful crumbled cheese

For the vinaigrette, combine the red wine, red wine vinegar, and honey in a small saucepan. Bring to a boil, lower the heat to a strong simmer, and reduce by half. Allow to cool to room temperature, then add the salt, pepper, and mustard; whisk until the salt dissolves. Add the olive oil in a slow steady stream, whisking all the while. Whisk until well emulsified and set aside. This can be done up to 4 hours before serving.

Preheat the oven to 425°F. Peel and core the tomatoes, then quarter them and remove the seeds. Cut the onion into wedges. In a bowl, gently mix the tomatoes, onion, 1 tablespoon chopped oregano, olive oil, sea salt, and pepper. Spread this mixture out in an even layer in a large ceramic baking dish. A Spanish earthenware dish called a *cazuela* would work well. Roast, stirring occasionally, for 15 to 20 minutes, until the juices from the tomatoes have evaporated and the edges of the vegetables have caramelized well. The tomatoes should reduce to a very concentrated, chunky puree.

To serve, cut 6 ($^1/_2$-inch-thick) slices of bread. Toast or grill the bread, and toss the arugula and chives with the vinaigrette. Smear the tomatoes liberally on the toasts. Sprinkle the greens over the tomatoes, crumble on some cheese (Spanish blue cheese or aged goat cheese is good), and finish with a sprinkle of minced oregano.

Roasted Artichokes with Tarragon-Basil Dipping Sauce

SERVES 6 TO 8

3 or 4 large artichokes

Poaching Liquid

12 cups water

2 cups white wine

$1/4$ cup lemon juice

1 small onion, diced

1 or 2 bay leaves

5 black peppercorns

3 coriander seeds

3 cloves garlic

2 tablespoons sea salt

$1^1/2$ cups sour cream

$1/2$ cup mayonnaise

$1^1/2$ teaspoons freshly squeezed lemon juice

$1/4$ bunch tarragon

$1/3$ bunch basil

1 small clove garlic

4 tablespoons olive oil

Sea salt and freshly ground black pepper

2 tablespoons butter

3 or 4 lemons

Cut off the top inch of each artichoke, and snip remaining tips off the leaves. Cut the stalks off about 1 inch from the bottom. Put all the poaching liquid ingredients in a large pot and bring to a boil. Add the artichokes, bring the water back to a boil, and immediately reduce to a simmer. Cook for 30 to 45 minutes, until the artichokes are tender at the heart (gently poke them with a fork to test for doneness). Remove them from the water and turn them upside down to drain and cool. Cut them in half lengthwise; scoop out and discard the feathery chokes. The artichokes can be held up to 24 hours.

Put the sour cream, mayonnaise, lemon juice, tarragon, basil, garlic, 2 tablespoons olive oil, and salt and pepper to taste in a food processor or blender and puree until the mixture is very thick and creamy. Cover and refrigerate.

About 20 minutes before serving, preheat the oven to 500°F. Heat the remaining olive oil and butter in a large ovenproof sauté pan until hot. Halve the lemons and add them cut side down. Add the artichokes, cut side up, and cook 1 minute, moving the artichokes to coat with oil. Season to taste with salt and pepper. Flip the artichokes over and cook for 2 to 3 minutes, until beginning to brown. Roast in the oven for 8 to 10 minutes, until the artichokes are caramelized. Serve hot with the lemons for squeezing over the artichokes and the dipping sauce.

Chorizo and Goat Cheese Half-Moons

SERVES 6

2 to 3 ounces of your favorite soft fresh goat cheese

12 to 18 (about 3 ounces) paper-thin slices chorizo or other sausage

1 egg

1 tablespoon water

Panko, for coating

Peanut oil or vegetable oil, for deep-frying

Put 1 teaspoon goat cheese on each sausage slice. Fold over to create half-moon shapes, and press to seal. Cover and refrigerate for at least 1 hour, or as long as overnight.

About 30 minutes before you're ready to cook the half-moons, mix the egg and water in one bowl and pour some panko into another. Dip each half-moon in the egg wash, then roll it in the panko, pressing to get an even coating and gently shaking off the excess. Chill for 30 minutes, or the coating will get soggy.

Heat $1/2$ inch oil to 375°F in a heavy straight-sided pot. Carefully add enough half-moons to fill but not overcrowd the pan. You want them to have room to move without touching. Cook about 1 minute on each side, until golden brown and crispy, then drain on paper towels. Skim any leftover bits and let the oil return to 375°F before frying the next batch. Serve immediately with toothpicks.

Black Pepper and Garlic Chicken Wings

SERVES 6

Marinade

1/2 cup mushroom soy sauce or regular soy sauce (substitute 1 tablespoon ketjap manis for 1 tablespoon of the soy sauce, if you have it)

2 tablespoons brown sugar or palm sugar

1 tablespoon honey

2 tablespoons minced garlic

2 tablespoons freshly ground black pepper

3 pounds chicken wings

Minced garlic, fresh chives, or scallions, for garnish

Combine all the marinade ingredients in a bowl and mix well.

Trim off and discard the wing tips, and cut each wing at the joint so you end up with 1 drumstick and 1 flat section per wing. Place the wings in a sealable plastic bag or a large flat plastic container and pour the marinade over, making sure that all surfaces are coated well. Close the bag tightly, and marinate in the refrigerator for 12 to 24 hours, shaking or turning the wings often.

Preheat the oven to 450°F. Arrange the wings on a rack in a shallow roasting pan. Roast for 12 to 18 minutes, until the skin is dark brown and crispy and the meat has begun to shrink away from the ends of the bones. The juices should run clear when the wings are pierced with a knife point. Sprinkle with the garnishes and serve them up!

Chicken Satay with Baby Greens

SERVES 6

Marinade

2 tablespoons Dijon mustard

2 tablespoons balsamic vinegar

1 tablespoon rice vinegar

6 tablespoons hoisin

1/2 teaspoon minced garlic

1/2 teaspoon minced peeled fresh ginger

2 teaspoons minced shallots

1 pound boneless, skinless chicken thighs

Juice and zest of 1 lemon

1 tablespoon Dijon mustard

1 teaspoon minced shallot

Pinch of sea salt

Freshly ground black pepper

6 to 8 tablespoons extra virgin olive oil

1 cup baby arugula

Soak 12 bamboo skewers in enough water to cover for at least 30 minutes.

Whisk together the marinade ingredients in a bowl. Set aside 2 tablespoons for basting. Cut the chicken into bite-size pieces. Put the chicken pieces in the marinade, turn to coat, cover, and refrigerate for 2 hours.

Combine the lemon juice, zest, mustard, shallot, salt, and pepper in a bowl, and mix well. Add the oil in a slow steady stream, whisking continuously until well emulsified. Set aside until needed.

Thread pieces of marinated chicken onto the skewers so that they are right next to each other but not scrunched up. Try to keep the chicken as flat as possible. Grill over a hot fire or in a hot grill pan, rotating a quarter turn halfway through cooking, for 1 1/2 to 2 minutes per side.

While the chicken is grilling, combine the greens and dress them with enough of the vinaigrette to coat. Arrange the arugula in the middle of each of 6 plates, lay 2 skewers of chicken across each, and serve.

Ken Hom's Pork Riblets

SERVES 6

Marinade

$^1/_2$ cup hoisin

$1^1/_2$ teaspoons sugar

$2^1/_4$ teaspoons tamari

$2^1/_4$ teaspoons sherry vinegar

$2^1/_4$ teaspoons rice vinegar

2 scallions, minced

$^1/_2$ teaspoon Tabasco

$^3/_4$ teaspoon black bean sauce or hot garlic sauce

$^3/_4$ teaspoon grated peeled fresh ginger

$2^1/_4$ teaspoons minced garlic

$^1/_2$ teaspoon pepper

2 tablespoons minced fresh cilantro

$1^1/_2$ teaspoons dark (Asian) sesame oil

$2^1/_2$ to 3 pounds spareribs, cut crosswide into $1^1/_2$ inch strips

Toasted sesame seeds

Thinly sliced scallions

Whisk together all the marinade ingredients in a stainless steel or ceramic bowl.

Put the ribs in a sealable plastic bag or a suitable container. Pour the marinade over, making sure all surfaces get coated well. Marinate in the refrigerator for 24 hours, shaking the bag or turning the ribs occasionally.

When ready to cook, remove the ribs from the refrigerator and bring them to room temperature. Preheat the oven to 300°F.

Transfer the ribs to a 1-inch-high rack in a roasting pan and brush with some of the marinade. Put $^1/_2$ inch of water in the bottom of the pan. Roast, covered, for 45 minutes, then turn the ribs over and roast 45 minutes longer. Remove from the oven and baste with marinade again. Increase the oven temperature to 400°F and roast for 10 minutes more per side (20 minutes total), until the meat is pulling away from the bone. Check several times as the ribs are roasting and add a small amount of water if they are getting too caramelized.

You can serve the ribs now while they are still hot and sticky, or let them cool and reheat later under the broiler or on a barbecue grill. To serve, cut the strips of ribs into individual riblets, and sprinkle liberally with the sesame seeds and scallions.

My Very First Beef Satay

SERVES 6

8 to 12 ounces flank
steak or skirt steak

Marinade

3 tablespoons tamari

1 tablespoon sugar

2 tablespoons dry sherry

1 tablespoon minced
peeled fresh ginger

1 clove garlic, minced

1 1/2 teaspoons dark
(Asian) sesame oil

Mustard Sauce

1/4 cup sugar

2 tablespoons Colman's
mustard powder

1 egg yolk

1/4 cup red wine vinegar

6 tablespoons crème
fraîche or sour cream

1 to 1 1/2 tablespoons
sesame seeds, toasted

Fresh cilantro leaves

Soak 6 long or 12 short (4 or 5-inch) bamboo skewers in enough water to cover for at least 30 minutes.

Trim the meat of excess fat, then poke it all over with a fork to tenderize it. Cut the meat across the grain into 12 slices, each about 1/4 inch thick, and put it in a sealable plastic bag or a shallow dish. Combine all the marinade ingredients and mix well. Pour the marinade over the meat and refrigerate for 2 hours.

Combine the sugar and mustard powder in the top of a double boiler and whisk thoroughly. Whisk in the egg yolk and vinegar and cook over simmering water, stirring occasionally, for 10 to 15 minutes, until the mixture is thick enough to form ribbons when drizzled from the spoon. Allow to cool, fold in crème fraîche, and refrigerate.

Thread the marinated steak onto skewers, 2 pieces each for long skewers, 1 piece for the short ones. Keep the meat as flat as you can for more even cooking. Grill over a hot charcoal or wood fire for 1 to 2 minutes per side, depending on the heat of your fire, until the meat is crisply caramelized on the edges and nicely browned, but still rare.

To serve, place a small bowl of the mustard sauce in the center of a platter and arrange the satays around it. Sprinkle the satays with sesame seeds and a bit of cilantro.

Baked Goat Cheese and Tomato Fondue

6 thin slices sturdy bread

2 pounds heirloom tomatoes, or 2 (16-ounce) cans diced tomatoes

2 tablespoons extra virgin olive oil

2 large shallots, sliced

4 cloves garlic, sliced

$1/4$ teaspoon kosher salt or sea salt

$1/8$ teaspoon freshly ground black pepper

1 fresh bay leaf (use Turkish bay, not California) or 1 sprig basil

2 tablespoons white wine

2 tablespoons sliced dates, prunes, or dried apricots

1 (9-ounce) jar Cabécou cheese (aged goat cheese), at room temperature

Cut the slices of bread in half. Grill, toast, or oven-toast them so they are nice and crispy. Set aside.

Peel and seed the tomatoes. If they are extremely juicy, set them in a colander to drain for 20 minutes or so, then chop them into $1/2$-inch pieces. (Canned tomatoes should be drained, too.) Heat the olive oil in a heavy wide pan over medium heat. Add the shallots and garlic and cook slowly for 8 to 10 minutes, until very tender. Increase the heat and add the tomatoes, salt, pepper, and bay leaf; cook for another 30 seconds or so. Add the wine and cook until it has evaporated. Add the fruit and take the pan off the heat. The dish can be held at this point and finished later.

Preheat the oven to 500°F. Cut the disks of cheese in half horizontally, making 6 small rounds. Spoon the tomatoes into a baking dish and top with the cheese. Bake for 6 to 8 minutes, until the top of the cheese is golden and the tomato sauce is heated through and looks rich and thick.

Set the baking dish on a napkin-lined plate (to keep it from sliding around) with the "croutons" alongside, so your guests can make their own toasts.

Morel and Goat Cheese Toasts

2 tablespoons extra
virgin olive oil

4 teaspoons unsalted
butter

2 shallots, thinly sliced
into rounds

4 cups fresh morel
mushrooms, quartered
lengthwise and carefully
cleaned

Kosher salt or sea salt
and freshly ground black
pepper

2 teaspoons chopped
fresh thyme leaves

1/4 cup Calvados,
Madeira, or Cognac

4 ounces fresh goat
cheese

2 tablespoons heavy
whipping cream or
half-and-half

6 (1/3-inch-thick) slices
rustic country bread

1/4 cup chopped fresh
flat-leaf parsley

Heat the olive oil and 2 teaspoons of the butter in a sauté pan over medium heat. Add the shallots and cook, stirring, for 3 to 5 minutes, until they begin to caramelize. Add the mushrooms and sauté, stirring occasionally, for 8 to 10 minutes, until tender. Sprinkle to taste with salt and pepper. When the mushrooms start to caramelize and give off their juices, add the thyme and sauté for 1 minute more. Then stir in the Calvados and the remaining 2 teaspoons butter and keep warm over low heat until you are ready to serve.

In a bowl, mix the cheese with the cream to make it spreadable. Toast or grill the bread, smear each slice with a nice layer of the creamy goat cheese, and place on serving plates. Pour the mushroom sauce over, sprinkle with parsley, and serve at once.

Asparagus and Truffle Butter Toasts

1 pound asparagus

3 slices highest-quality rustic whole wheat bread

1 tablespoon unsalted butter

$^1/_3$ cup water

$^3/_4$ teaspoon sea salt

$^1/_4$ teaspoon freshly ground black pepper

$1^1/_2$ ounces black truffle butter

2 tablespoons chopped fresh herbs, such as flat-leaf parsley, tarragon, or chives

Snap off the tough ends of the asparagus spears where they break naturally. Slice the asparagus diagonally into $1^1/_2$-inch pieces.

Toast the bread, cut the slices in half, and keep warm in the oven.

Melt the unsalted butter in a sauté pan over low heat until foamy. Add the asparagus and increase the heat to medium-high. Cook for several minutes, shaking the pan until the asparagus is thoroughly covered with butter. Add the water, salt, and pepper and bring to a boil. Cook for 2 or 3 more minutes, until the water is evaporated and the asparagus is done to your liking (test a piece).

In a small pan, melt the truffle butter over low heat until foamy and slightly browned.

Toss the herbs into the asparagus and mix well. Divide the asparagus equally among the 6 pieces of toast and drizzle with truffle butter. Serve while hot.

Summer King Salmon Kebabs

Vinaigrette

1 tablespoon Champagne vinegar

3 tablespoons extra virgin olive oil

1 to 2 tablespoons finely chopped fresh dill weed, fennel fronds, or chives

Kosher salt or sea salt and freshly ground black pepper

1 tablespoon sesame seeds

1 tablespoon yellow mustard seeds

1 tablespoon brown mustard seeds

12 ounces king salmon fillets, small bones removed and cut into 6 equal rectangular pieces

1/4 cup Dijon mustard

1 1/2 cups loosely packed mizuna, arugula, or frisée

Soak 6 (4 to 5-inch) bamboo skewers in enough water to cover for at least 30 minutes. (Try to get those flat Japanese bamboo skewers.)

Combine the vinaigrette ingredients and whisk until emulsified.

Toast the sesame seeds in a dry pan, shaking them all the while, until aromatic and lightly golden, and put them in a small bowl. Toast the mustard seeds the same way, but cover the pan: mustard seeds toast faster and also pop all over the place. Combine with sesame seeds and allow to cool. Stir, then set aside half the seeds. Finely grind the rest of the seeds, and spread the powder out on a plate.

Smear the flesh of the salmon (not the skin) with mustard. Firmly press the salmon, mustard side down, into the ground seeds to coat. Now thread the fish onto the skewers, keeping the pieces as flat as possible.

Grill the kebabs for 1 1/2 minutes per side for medium-rare, or pan-sear for 1 1/2 minutes per side over high heat in a cast iron skillet coated with a little olive oil. For skinless salmon, pan-searing works better—be sure to crust both sides.

Very lightly dress the greens with the vinaigrette and divide among 6 small plates. Lay the kebabs on top of the greens, drizzle with additional vinaigrette, and sprinkle with reserved whole seeds.

Grilled Oysters—Easy as Pie

SERVES 6

Cindy's Barbecue Sauce

$^1/_2$ cup barbecue sauce (your favorite brand)

$^1/_2$ cup freshly squeezed lemon juice

1 tablespoon Worcestershire sauce

1 teaspoon freshly ground black pepper

Tiny pinch of cayenne pepper

Soy-Lime Sauce

4 tablespoons tamari

2 tablespoons freshly squeezed lime juice

18 to 24 fresh oysters

Tabasco sauce, for serving

Lime wedges, for serving

Fine sea salt

Freshly ground black pepper

For the barbecue sauce, combine all the ingredients in a small saucepan. Bring this mixture just to a boil, remove from the heat, and reserve in the pan. You will need to reheat this sauce before serving and, when you do, try to time it so it is hot just as the oysters are coming off the grill.

For the sauce, combine the tamari and lime juice in a squirt bottle and shake well.

Prepare a hot fire in the grill. Carefully shuck the oysters, leaving each oyster and as much of its juices as possible in the cupped bottom shell. To grill, place the oysters on the grill and cook for 30 seconds to 1 minute, until the juice in the shells gets bubbly and the edges of the oysters are just beginning to curl. Take care not to overcook them: you want a bit of the natural juices left around the oysters when you pull them off the grill. (If you are not into shucking oysters, just give them a good scrub beforehand. Put the whole oysters on the grill to cook, and they'll automatically pop open when they're done. Discard any that do not open when cooked.)

Reheat the barbecue sauce if necessary and set it out, along with the squeeze bottle of Soy-Lime Sauce (give it a good shake) and—for those who like to season their oysters as they do in Mexico—the Tabasco sauce, lime wedges, salt, and pepper. Dressing the oysters is a do-it-yourself thing that should be done while the oysters are still hot—or while they're still on the grill, just before you pull them off.

Orange, Tomato, and Chile Manila Clams or Mussels

SERVES 4

36 Manila clams or mussels

4 thick slices rustic country bread

Extra virgin olive oil from roasted garlic (see page 17), for brushing

1 tablespoon olive oil

10 cloves garlic, sliced

2 tablespoons grated peeled fresh ginger

Finely grated zest and juice of 1 orange

3 tomatoes, peeled, seeded, and minced

1/2 cup dry white wine

1/4 cup unsalted butter

3 tablespoons chopped fresh basil, dill, or other herbs

1/2 teaspoon sea salt

1/4 teaspoon freshly ground black pepper

Pinch of dried chile flakes

Scrub the shellfish thoroughly under cool running water. If you're using mussels, trim away any beards.

Preheat a grill. Brush 1 side of the bread with the roasted garlic oil and grill, oil side down, until nice grill marks appear.

Heat the 1 tablespoon olive oil in a large, deep sauté pan with a cover over high heat. (Use 2 pans if you don't have one large enough to hold all the shellfish at once.) Add the garlic and ginger and sauté for 30 seconds. Add the clams, and toss for 2 minutes more. Add the orange juice, tomatoes, and wine. Cover and cook over medium-high heat for 6 to 8 minutes, until the clams or mussels open. Uncover, raise the heat, and add the butter, basil, orange zest, salt, pepper, and chile flakes. Cook until the butter is melted and the juices have thickened somewhat.

Transfer the shellfish to a plate, discarding any that have still not opened, and reduce the broth over high heat a bit more, if desired. Pour the broth over the shellfish. Serve with the grilled bread.

Grilled Figs with Pancetta and Walnuts

SERVES 6 to 8

24 large fresh figs

24 very thinly sliced strips pancetta

Vinaigrette

2 tablespoons balsamic vinegar

2 tablespoons sherry vinegar

$1/2$ teaspoon sea salt

$1/4$ teaspoon freshly ground black pepper

$3/4$ cup olive oil

1 tablespoon shredded fresh basil leaves

1 tablespoon shredded fresh mint leaves

1 tablespoon minced fresh chives

Extra virgin olive oil

Sea salt and freshly ground black pepper

2 cups walnut pieces, toasted

$1/4$ cup thinly sliced (diagonally) scallions

Fresh mint leaves

Soak 6 to 8 (8-inch) bamboo skewers (twice as many if the figs are large) in enough water to cover for at least 30 minutes. Wrap each fig in a strip of pancetta, and thread 3 or 4 figs onto a skewer, securing the pancetta with the skewer. For large figs, use 2 skewers, placed parallel to each other. Prepare the skewers several hours ahead of time, and refrigerate them on a baking sheet. They handle better when chilled.

For the vinaigrette, whisk together the vinegars, salt, and pepper in a small bowl, until the salt dissolves. Gradually whisk in the olive oil, continue to whisk until fully emulsified, then whisk in the basil, mint, and chives.

When you're ready to serve, brush the figs with olive oil and sprinkle with salt and pepper to taste. Grill until the fat on the pancetta is rendered and the figs are golden brown and lightly caramelized.

Drizzle the figs with the vinaigrette, sprinkle the walnuts and scallions around, garnish with the mint leaves, and enjoy.

Pablo's Boquerones

1/3 cup finely sliced plump (oil-packed) sun-dried tomatoes

1/2 cup finely shaved or julienned fennel bulb

1 to 2 tablespoons torn fennel fronds

1 tablespoon aged Spanish sherry vinegar

Kosher salt or sea salt

Freshly ground black pepper

3 tablespoons Spanish extra virgin olive oil

18 to 30 boquerones (fillets of white anchovy)

1/3 cup 1/4-inch-diced croutons (optional)

1 shallot, minced or cut into thin circles and separated

1 or 2 piquillo chiles, finely sliced, or 1/2 cup finely sliced roasted red bell pepper

1 tablespoon minced fresh thyme leaves

Combine the sun-dried tomatoes and the fennel bulb and fronds in a small bowl. Combine the vinegar, a tiny pinch of salt (remember that the fish are salty), and pepper to taste in another small bowl, stir until the salt has dissolved, then gradually whisk in the oil.

When you are ready to serve, place 3 to 5 *boquerones* around each of 6 small plates. Lightly dress the sun-dried tomatoes and fennel with vinaigrette and sprinkle them over the anchovies so the anchovies still show. Over that go the croutons, shallot, chiles, and thyme. Finish with a drizzle of the remaining dressing and a few grindings of black pepper.

Duck, Olive, and Fig Skewers

Marinade

2 tablespoons chopped
fresh herbs

$1/4$ teaspoon sea salt

$1/8$ teaspoon freshly
ground black pepper

2 tablespoons olive oil

2 tablespoons white wine

3 duck breasts, skin
removed, cut into
18 equal pieces

1 tablespoon highest-
quality balsamic vinegar

$1/4$ teaspoon sea salt

Pinch of freshly ground
black pepper

3 tablespoons extra
virgin olive oil

6 to 12 green olives,
pitted

6 to 12 fresh figs,
apricots, or peaches,
halved

1 lemon, cut into
6 wedges (optional)

Whisk the marinade ingredients together in a small bowl. Place the duck breasts in a sealable plastic bag or a suitable container. Pour the marinade over, making sure all surfaces are well coated. Marinate in the refrigerator for 3 to 24 hours.

Combine the vinegar, salt, and pepper in a small bowl, and mix well. Drizzle in the olive oil, whisking as you go. Continue whisking until well emulsified. Reserve until needed.

Thread the marinated duck onto 6 (6-inch) skewers, alternating 3 duck pieces with the olives and/or figs (you can use 2 olives, 2 figs, or 1 of each). Using a cast iron grill pan or grill, grill over medium-high heat for about 2 minutes per side for medium-rare meat. Drizzle 2 to 3 teaspoons of the vinaigrette over each skewer before serving.

Garnish with a lemon wedge and serve.

Baby Zucchini with Garden Herbs

SERVES 6

2 pounds baby
(4 to 5-inch) zucchini

1 tablespoon minced
fresh oregano or savory
leaves

1 tablespoon minced
fresh thyme or flat-leaf
parsley leaves

2 tablespoons extra
virgin olive oil

Kosher salt or sea salt
and freshly ground black
pepper

2 tablespoons unsalted
butter, melted

Coarse sea salt,
preferably French gray
sea salt or Maldon flake
salt

Minced oregano, savory,
thyme, or parsley to
finish (optional)

Trim off the tough ends and split the zucchini in half length-wise (or leave whole if very small). Mix the oregano and thyme with the olive oil. Season the zucchini with salt and pepper to taste, then brush with the oil mixture.

Grill over medium coals for about 1 minute, cut side down, then turn and grill the other side for about 1 minute, until tender.

To serve, brush with the butter and sprinkle with sea salt. You can sprinkle with additional herbs, if desired.

Goat Cheese–Stuffed Gypsy Peppers

SERVES 6

6 gypsy peppers or small bell peppers

³/₄ cup cream cheese

1¹/₂ cups feta cheese

2 cups cooked basmati rice, chilled

³/₄ cup golden raisins

¹/₃ cup chopped mint

Vinaigrette

1 to 1¹/₂ pints cherry tomatoes, halved

2 to 3 tablespoons minced fresh basil

1 tablespoon minced flat-leaf parsley leaves

3 tablespoons rice vinegar

1 tablespoon freshly squeezed lemon juice

¹/₂ teaspoon sea salt

¹/₄ teaspoon freshly ground black pepper

6 tablespoons extra virgin olive oil

¹/₄ cup sliced almonds, toasted

2 to 3 tablespoons crème fraîche

Cut around the base of each pepper stem and gently pull the stem out. Trim off the seeds and keep the tops to hold the stuffing in. Blanch the peppers in boiling water for 60 to 90 seconds, until just tender. Drain and shock in an ice bath. Drain again very well before stuffing.

Fit a stand mixer with the paddle attachment and beat the cream cheese until light and fluffy. Crumble in the feta cheese and beat until well mixed. Quickly mix in the rice, raisins, and mint, breaking up any raisins that are sticking together.

Divide the filling into 6 equal portions. Moisten your hands, then roll each into a lozenge about the same shape as the peppers. Slip the lozenges into the peppers, pressing them gently to get the filling into all the nooks and crannies. Put the tops back on and set the peppers aside.

Combine the cherry tomatoes, basil, and parsley in a bowl. In a small bowl, whisk together the vinegar, lemon juice, salt, and pepper until the salt is dissolved. Whisk in the olive oil, then pour over the tomatoes and herbs and mix gently. The vinaigrette should be mixed no more than 20 minutes or so in advance of serving.

Grill the peppers over a medium-high flame until caramelized nicely on all sides and hot through. To serve, place a few spoonfuls of vinaigrette on each of 6 plates. Top with a stuffed pepper, sprinkle with almonds, and drizzle with crème fraîche.

Grilled Yams and Potatoes with Harissa

SERVES 6

Harissa

8 serrano chiles

2 teaspoons cumin seeds, toasted and ground

4 cloves garlic, minced

2 tablespoons paprika

1 teaspoon cayenne pepper

$^1/_2$ cup extra virgin olive oil

2 tablespoons freshly squeezed lemon juice

Kosher salt or sea salt

Grated zest and juice of $^1/_2$ lemon

1 shallot, minced

Sea salt

Black pepper

Extra virgin olive oil

2 large yams

6 small to medium Yukon gold potatoes, halved

$^1/_4$ cup plain yogurt

3 tablespoons minced fresh flat-leaf parsley

Mince the chiles and mix in a small bowl with all the remaining harissa ingredients, including salt to taste. Refrigerate, and warm gently before serving.

Whisk together the lemon zest and juice, shallot, a pinch of salt, and a pinch of pepper in a small bowl until the salt is dissolved. Gradually whisk in 3 or 4 tablespoons of olive oil, and continue to whisk until fully emulsified.

Preheat the oven to 375°F. Wash the yams and potatoes well and rub them with some olive oil. Prick the yams with a fork. Place on a baking sheet and bake for 35 to 45 minutes, until a skewer can just barely go to the center. Allow the yams and potatoes to cool until you can handle them. Then, without peeling them, cut diagonally into $^1/_2$-inch-thick slices.

Brush the slices lightly with olive oil, season with salt and pepper to taste, and place on a grill (an oak fire is good). Rotating a quarter turn on each side to get nice crosshatch grill marks, grill for no more than 2 minutes, until heated through.

To serve, arrange 3 slices of yam alternately with 3 slices of potato on individual plates. Drizzle with 1 or 2 teaspoons vinaigrette, and sprinkle on a few drops of harissa. Top with a drizzle of yogurt and a scattering of chopped parsley. The leftover harissa is great on grilled tuna and swordfish, and scrambled eggs.

Miso-Glazed Beef in Lettuce Cups

SERVES 6

2½ tablespoons sake

2½ tablespoons mirin

1½ teaspoons sugar

⅓ cup shiro miso

12 ounces beef tenderloin

⅛ teaspoon sea salt

⅛ teaspoon pepper

8 ounces asparagus

¾ cup watercress

12 shiso leaves

1 (6-inch) piece daikon

Vinaigrette

2 tablespoons rice vinegar

1 teaspoon sugar

1½ teaspoons soy sauce

¼ cup peanut oil

⅛ teaspoon dark (Asian) sesame oil

Tiny pinch of sea salt

12 butter lettuce leaves

Combine the sake, mirin, and sugar in a small saucepan and bring to a boil. Remove from the heat, add the miso, and stir.

Cut the meat into 6 cubes or rectangles. Season with the salt and pepper, and coat it well with the marinade. Marinate for 2 to 4 hours in the refrigerator.

Snap off the ends of the asparagus and blanch them for 1 to 2 minutes. Refrigerate to cool. Cut into bite-size pieces. Mix the asparagus, watercress, and shiso in a bowl and set aside. Peel the daikon and shred it into long strips with a vegetable peeler into a separate bowl and set aside.

Combine the vinegar and sugar in a small saucepan. Heat and stir just until the sugar has dissolved. Remove from heat, add the remaining vinaigrette ingredients, and whisk until well emulsified. Set aside until needed.

Grill the meat over a hot fire for about 2 minutes per side for rare, a little longer if you prefer. Baste with the marinade as you go, and rotate the meat a quarter turn halfway through cooking on each side to get nice crosshatch grill marks.

Cut the beef into thin slices. Dress the asparagus mixture with just enough vinaigrette to moisten. Place a small amount of the asparagus mixture, some daikon, and some beef in each lettuce leaf. Sprinkle any remaining vegetables about, drizzle a little vinaigrette over the cups, and serve the rest on the side.

Crispy Black Bean-Rice Cakes

SERVES 6

2 cups well-drained cooked black beans (or one 15-ounce can, drained)

$3/4$ cup cooked basmati rice

$1/2$ cup finely chopped red onion

$1/2$ bunch scallions, white and a bit of the green parts, minced

1 to $1^1/2$ jalapeño chiles, seeded and minced

$1/4$ bunch cilantro leaves, minced

$1/2$ teaspoon kosher salt or sea salt

$1/4$ teaspoon freshly ground black pepper

1 to 2 tablespoons unsalted butter

Sour cream, for serving

Freshly squeezed lime juice or salsa, for serving

Put half of the beans and half of the rice in a food processor and pulse several times until coarsely chopped and well mixed. Combine the onion, scallions, chiles, cilantro, salt, and pepper in a large bowl, add the processed beans and rice, and stir well. Alternatively, eliminate the food processor step and mash up everything with a potato masher or strong whisk.

Scoop out $1/2$-cup portions and, with wet hands, shape them into 6 patties about $3/4$ inch thick and 3 inches in diameter. Use a griddle or a heavy pan big enough to hold all the cakes and with room to get a spatula around them. Melt 1 tablespoon of the butter over medium heat. When the butter is foamy and begins to brown, add the cakes. Cook for 2 to 3 minutes. When the bottoms are nice and crispy, flip the cakes over and cook the other side for 2 to 3 more minutes, until nice and crispy, adding more butter if needed. Serve warm, topped with a dollop of sour cream and a squeeze of lime juice or salsa.

Crab Cakes with Red Beet Rémoulade

1 bunch small beets

Extra virgin olive oil

1 pound potatoes

1 tablespoon rice vinegar

2 tablespoons Dijon mustard

2 to 3 tablespoons grated horseradish

1/2 teaspoon pepper

1 pound crabmeat

1 red bell pepper, roasted, peeled, seeded, and minced

3 scallions, minced

3 tablespoons minced fresh parsley

1/2 jalapeño, minced

1 egg

6 to 7 tablespoons mayonnaise

2 teaspoons sea salt

1/2 to 3/4 cup freshly toasted bread crumbs

Lemon wedges

Chervil sprigs

Preheat the oven to 375°F. Trim the beets, leaving 1 inch of the stem intact, but do not peel. Lightly coat with olive oil and bake until fork tender. In a separate pan, bake the potatoes until fork tender. Allow the potatoes to cool, then peel and finely grate. Set aside. Allow the beets to cool, then peel and grate enough to measure 1 cup. Save any leftover beets for salads. Whisk together the vinegar, mustard, and 1/4 cup of olive oil, then stir in the 1 cup beets, horseradish to taste, and 1/4 teaspoon of the pepper. Refrigerate.

Combine the crabmeat, grated potatoes, bell pepper, scallions, parsley, jalapeño, egg, 6 tablespoons mayonnaise, salt, and 1/4 teaspoon of pepper. Mix gently. Add more mayonnaise if the mixture seems too dry. Sprinkle 1/2 cup of the bread crumbs over the mixture and combine gently, adding more, until the mixture just holds together. Refrigerate for 20 minutes or up to several hours.

When the crab mixture is well chilled, make 12 small cakes of equal thickness (at least 3/8 inch). Coat the surface on a non-stick skillet with oil and place over medium-high heat. When hot, add the crab cakes in batches, being careful not to crowd the pan. Cook for about 7 minutes, until golden brown and crisp on one side. Cook on the second side for about 5 minutes, until browned. Keep warm in a low oven.

Divide the crab cakes among serving plates and the rémoulade. Serve with lemon wedges and chervil sprigs.

Potato-Leek Pancakes with Sour Cream and Chives

SERVES 6

2 large russet potatoes

1 leek, white and light green parts only, sliced into thin circles and rinsed

1 teaspoon kosher salt or sea salt

$1/2$ to $3/4$ teaspoon freshly ground black pepper, plus additional for serving

2 to 3 tablespoons unsalted butter, duck or goose fat, butter and olive oil combined, or vegetable oil

$1/2$ to $3/4$ cup sour cream or crème fraîche

$1/2$ bunch chives, finely chopped

Peel and grate the potatoes, and put them into cold water. Drain the potatoes and squeeze out the excess water. Pat the leeks dry. In a bowl, mix the potatoes and leeks, then mix in the salt and pepper. In a large cast iron or nonstick pan or griddle over medium-high heat, melt enough of the butter to coat the pan. Working in batches, place small portions (about 2 tablespoonfuls) of the mixture in the pan and press with the back of a spatula to flatten. Add more butter as needed to keep the pan greased. Cook for about 2 minutes, until golden brown on the underside, then flip and cook the other side, for about 2 minutes, until golden brown.

To serve, place dollops of sour cream on the pancakes and top with the chives and sprinkle with pepper.

Grape and Almond Gazpacho

Soup

2 pounds seedless green grapes

1 small cucumber, peeled, seeded, and coarsely chopped

$1/4$ cup almonds, toasted

2 scallions, white and light green parts only, coarsely chopped

$1/4$ cup rice vinegar

$1/2$ cup plain yogurt

3 ounces cream cheese

2 tablespoons extra virgin olive oil

$1/4$ cup buttermilk

$1/2$ teaspoon sea salt

$1/4$ teaspoon freshly ground white pepper

2 sprigs dill, minced

$1/8$ to $1/4$ teaspoon cayenne pepper

Minced fresh chives

Thin peeled cucumber slices

To make the soup, combine the grapes, cucumber, almonds, scallions, vinegar, yogurt, cream cheese, olive oil, and buttermilk in a blender or food processor. Process until almost smooth, with just a bit of texture remaining. Stir in the salt, pepper, dill weed, and cayenne until incorporated. Cover and refrigerate until cold.

To serve, ladle the cold soup into well-chilled bowls and garnish with the chives and cucumber slices.

Golden Beet Borscht with Dill Crème Fraîche

SERVES 6 TO 8

2 tablespoons olive oil

$1/2$ onion, finely diced

$1^1/2$ teaspoons sugar

1 tablespoon red wine vinegar

1 small carrot, peeled and minced

4 golden beets, roasted or boiled, peeled, and coarsely grated

1 teaspoon sea salt

$1/2$ teaspoon freshly ground black pepper

2 tablespoons minced flat-leaf parsley

$2^1/2$ cups Light Chicken Stock (page 99) or Vegetable Stock (page 98)

Dill Crème Fraîche

$1/3$ cup crème fraîche

1 tablespoon minced fresh dill weed

$1/4$ teaspoon kosher salt or sea salt

Heat a frying pan and coat with olive oil. Add the onion and cook for about 6 minutes, until soft, stirring so they don't become brown and are just beginning to lightly caramelize. When the onion begins to turn golden, but before it gets too brown, stir in the sugar and vinegar. Cook for another 5 to 8 minutes, until the liquid has evaporated, then add the carrot, and cook until it is thoroughly coated with the oil mixture. Add the beets, salt, pepper, parsley, and stock. Simmer for 15 to 20 minutes, until the vegetables are tender.

In the meantime, for the sauce, mix the crème fraîche, dill weed, and salt thoroughly in a small bowl.

Serve the borsht in small bowls or cups, ladling about $2^1/2$ to 3 ounces into each. Scoop a teaspoon or so of the crème fraîche mixture on top, adding more if desired.

Garlic Soup

SERVES 6

1 whole head garlic

2 tablespoons extra
virgin olive oil

1 leek, white and light
green parts only, well
rinsed and finely sliced

2 sprigs fresh thyme

2 small potatoes, cut into
1/2-inch dice

2 1/2 to 3 cups Light
Chicken Stock (page 99)
or water

Sea salt

Freshly ground black
pepper

1/4 cup cream (optional)

Garnish Options

Minced garlic chives and
chive blossoms

Toasted almond slices

Finely grated hard-boiled
egg

Minced parsley leaves
with a drizzle of truffle oil

Sprigs of thyme

Break up the head of garlic by pressing down on it with the heel of your hand or the broad side of a knife. Separate the cloves and cut off the root ends, then peel and slice the garlic. In a small saucepan, heat the oil over medium-low heat, add the leek and thyme, and sweat slowly until soft, 5 to 10 minutes or longer—the slower, the better. Add the garlic, increase the heat to medium, and cook, stirring often, till softened. Take care not to let the garlic brown.

Add the potatoes and stock and simmer until the potatoes are soft, 10 to 15 minutes. Remove the thyme and season to taste with salt and pepper. You may serve as is or, for a more elegant finish, put the soup in a blender, add the cream, and process until smooth. Reheat the soup if it has cooled too much. Sprinkle each serving with one of the garnish options, if desired.

Lamb Meatballs with Yogurt-Mint Sauce

MAKES 24 MEATBALLS

Sauce

1 cup plain Greek-style yogurt

$1/4$ cup minced scallions

$1^1/2$ tablespoons minced fresh mint

$1/2$ teaspoon salt

$1/4$ teaspoon piment d'Espelette (Basque chile powder)

$1/4$ teaspoon paprika

$1/4$ teaspoon piment d'Espelette

$1/4$ teaspoon freshly ground black pepper

$1/8$ teaspoon cinnamon

$3/4$ teaspoon sea salt

$1^1/4$ teaspoons chopped fresh mint

$1^1/2$ teaspoons chopped fresh oregano

8 ounces ground lamb

12 ounces ground beef

1 egg

1 ($3/4$-ounce) slice rustic country bread, soaked in water and squeezed dry

Put all the sauce ingredients in a bowl and mix thoroughly. Keep refrigerated while you prepare the meatballs.

Combine the paprika, *piment d'Espelette*, black pepper, cinnamon, and salt in a small bowl. Mix the spice mixture well, stirring in the mint and oregano.

Place the lamb and beef in a large bowl, add the egg, and mix well with your hands. Add the bread, making sure to distribute it evenly in the meat mixture. Dust with the spice mixture and mix.

Shape the meat into 1-tablespoon-size balls. Flatten each ball slightly and make a small indent on the top to hold the sauce. Heat a frying pan, coat with a small amount of olive oil, and cook several meatballs at a time, for 5 to 7 minutes, gently turning them to brown all sides. Alternatively, grill the meatballs for 2 minutes in a cast iron grill pan or over a gas or charcoal grill. Keep warm in the oven while you prepare the others.

To serve, spoon about $1/2$ to $3/4$ tablespoon of the sauce onto each meatball.

Sunday Supper Burgers

SERVES 6

Dressing

$1/2$ cup mayonnaise

$1/4$ cup pickle relish

2 to 3 tablespoons ketchup

3 or 4 drops Tabasco

1 drop Worcestershire

1 tablespoon chopped flat-leaf parsley leaves

1 tablespoon Cognac

2 strips bacon

2 large onions

12 to 14 ounces (18 percent fat) ground beef

Kosher salt or sea salt

Freshly ground black pepper

$1/2$ cup grated sharp Cheddar cheese

6 poppy seed brioche buns or 12 Black Pepper Mini Biscuits (page 13)

1 cup arugula

6 slices bread-and-butter pickles

1 tablespoon minced scallion

Combine all the dressing ingredients and mix well. Cover and refrigerate until needed.

Cut the bacon crosswise into 1-inch strips. Cook the bacon until crisp, transfer to a layer of paper towels, and set aside. Slice the onions into $1/4$-inch-thick rings, and pick out the small rings in the center that will fit snugly on top of the little burgers. You'll need a couple of rings per burger. Set these aside, too.

Form 6 or 12 small burger patties (depending on what size buns you are using) and season them with salt and pepper. Final preparation goes quickly, so line up everything you'll need before you get started cooking—dressing, bacon, onion rings, cheese, buns, arugula, pickles, and scallion. Cook the burgers over high heat, for 1 minute on each side for rare, or longer if desired. Remove from the heat, and immediately pile a tablespoon of cheese on each burger. After the cheese melts, top each with a couple of onion rings.

While the cheese is melting on the burgers, cut the buns in half, toast them, and generously spread some dressing on the bottoms. Top with some arugula, then the burgers, and then some pickles. Finally, sprinkle on a spoonful of bacon and a few scallion bits, and close off with the bun tops.

Porcini Mushroom Pot Pies

2 pounds fresh porcini mushrooms, chopped

2 red spring onions, cut into 6 pieces

Several sprigs thyme

$1^{1}/_{2}$ teaspoons sea salt

$^{1}/_{2}$ teaspoon freshly ground black pepper

3 tablespoons butter, at room temperature

1 tablespoon flour

$^{1}/_{2}$ cup minced onion

2 tablespoons Madeira

3 cups Mushroom Stock (page 100)

2 carrots, peeled, blanched, and cut into $1^{1}/_{2}$-inch pieces

$^{1}/_{2}$ cup heavy cream

2 tablespoons black truffle butter or unsalted butter

2 yams, baked until tender

3 tablespoons finely grated Parmesan cheese

2 tablespoons olive oil

1 tablespoon chopped fresh dill

Preheat the oven to 375°F. Combine the mushrooms, red onions, thyme, salt, and pepper in a baking dish just large enough to hold them in 1 layer. Roast for 20 to 30 minutes.

In a small bowl, mix 1 tablespoon of the butter thoroughly with the flour. Sauté the white onion with the remaining 2 tablespoons butter in a large pot over high heat for 6 to 8 minutes, stirring, until caramelized. Add the Madeira and cook until the liquid has evaporated. Stir in the stock and flour mixture, whisking until it comes to a strong boil. Cook for several minutes, or until the sauce begins to thicken. Add the carrots and mushroom mixture and boil for several more minutes, allowing the flavors to meld.

In a small pot, boil the cream and black truffle butter over medium-high heat for 3 to 5 minutes, until bubbly and reduced enough to coat a spoon.

Place the yams in an electric mixer and slowly pour in the cream mixture, beating until fluffy and smooth.

Scoop $^{3}/_{4}$ to 1 cup of the mushroom sauce into 6 to 8 individual size ovenproof bowls. Place a dollop of the yam mixture on top of each, spreading it out but leaving a $^{1}/_{4}$-inch or so rim open for the sauce to bubble up. Lightly sprinkle the cheese over the yams. Arrange the bowls on a baking sheet and bake for 35 to 40 minutes, until the crust is brown and bubbles of sauce are creeping out. Garnish with olive oil and dill.

Black Olive and Rainbow Chard Bars

7 ounces puff pastry dough, thawed if frozen

2 tablespoons olive oil

1 shallot, sliced

6 ounces rainbow chard, sliced into ribbons

$1/2$ teaspoon kosher salt or sea salt

$1/4$ teaspoon freshly ground black pepper

$1/2$ cup crème fraîche

1 egg

$1/2$ cup (2 ounces) freshly grated Parmesan cheese

$1/2$ cup pitted black olives, coarsely chopped

Preheat the oven to 400°F. Roll out the dough about $1/4$ inch thick and line an $8^1/2$ by 12-inch tart pan or baking pan, or place on a baking sheet. Chill in the refrigerator.

Heat a frying pan and coat with the olive oil. Add the shallot and chard. Cook for 1 or 2 minutes, until the chard has wilted slightly, then stir in the salt and pepper. Transfer the chard mixture to a baking sheet, making sure to spread it out, and chill in the refrigerator.

Remove the dough from the refrigerator and line or cover with aluminum foil, leaving a 1-inch edge (the pastry will puff up around the edges where it's not weighed down). Cover the foil with weights and bake for 15 to 20 minutes.

In the meantime, combine the crème fraîche, egg, and cheese in a bowl and mix well.

Remove the dough from the oven and take off the weights and foil. Spread the chard mixture evenly over the dough and sprinkle the olives on top. Smear the cheese mixture over the olives and chard, making sure to thoroughly cover these layers.

Return the pan to the oven and bake for 20 to 30 minutes, depending on your oven, until the cheese turns golden brown and the crust is a rich brown. Cool on a rack for 10 minutes before slicing into bars. Serve warm.

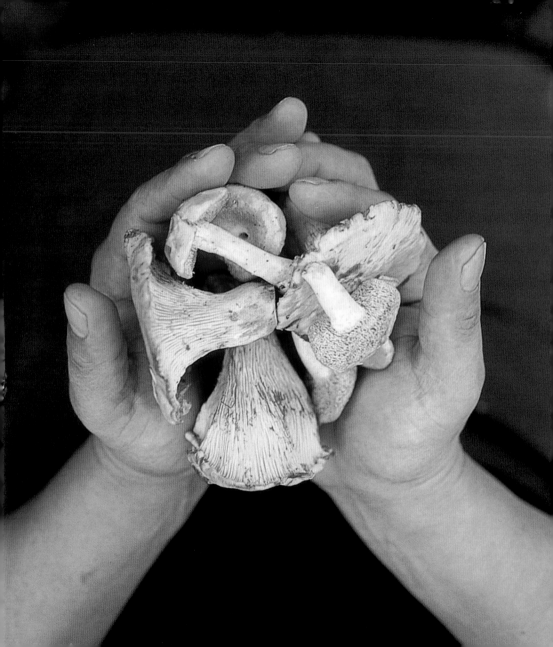

Parsnip and Mushroom Lasagne

SERVES 6

3 parsnips

1 carrot

1/2 onion, sliced

3 cups fresh wild or exotic mushrooms

1/4 cup olive oil

1 clove garlic, minced

3/4 teaspoon sea salt

1/4 teaspoon freshly ground black pepper

2 teaspoons fresh thyme

Sauce

2 cups heavy cream

3 to 4 tablespoons sherry

1/2 teaspoon sea salt

1/4 teaspoon pepper

1/8 teaspoon nutmeg

6 cooked lasagna noodles

4 1/2 ounces grated fontina

6 tablespoons ricotta

3 ounces grated Parmesan

Preheat the oven to 375°F. Lightly butter or oil 6 ramekins and arrange on a baking sheet.

Peel and slice the parsnips and carrot. Combine the parsnips, carrot, onion, mushrooms, and olive oil in a large bowl and mix thoroughly. Add the garlic, salt, pepper, and thyme, stirring in well. Spread the parsnip mixture in a large roasting pan or baking sheet, creating a thin layer. Bake for 30 to 45 minutes, until caramelized and tender.

For the sauce, bring the sauce ingredients to a boil in a saucepan, whisking. Pour 2 tablespoons of sauce into each ramekin, then add 2 tablespoons of the parsnip mixture.

Cut or break the lasagna noodles in half and place one half over the parsnip mixture. Layer on the cheeses next, placing 1 tablespoon fontina cheese, 1 tablespoon ricotta cheese, and 1 tablespoon Parmesan cheese into each dish. Add another 2 tablespoons sauce, 2 tablespoons parsnip mixture, the remaining half of the noodles, 1 tablespoon fontina cheese and 1 tablespoon Parmesan cheese (you will use all of the ricotta in the first layer).

Bake for 20 to 30 minutes, until lightly browned and bubbly. Let it rest for a few minutes before serving.

Vegetable Stock

MAKES ABOUT
4 QUARTS

1 tablespoon extra virgin olive oil

3 onions, chopped

3 carrots, peeled and chopped

2 stalks celery, chopped

5 cloves garlic, crushed

1 cup chopped cabbage

1 head romaine lettuce, chopped

1 leek, white and light green parts only, chopped

1 baking potato, peeled and chopped

2 tomatoes, chopped

Several sprigs flat-leaf parsley

Several sprigs thyme

Several sprigs basil or sage

1 tablespoon freshly cracked black peppercorns

1 teaspoon kosher salt or sea salt

6 to 8 quarts cold water

Heat the oil in a stockpot over medium heat. Add the onions, carrots, celery, and garlic and cook, stirring occasionally, for 8 to 10 minutes, until caramelized. If your pot is on the small side, you may want to brown the vegetables in several batches so you don't end up steaming them. Add all the remaining ingredients and bring to a boil. Reduce the heat to a simmer and cook, skimming often, for 45 to 60 minutes. Strain through a fine-mesh sieve and refrigerate until needed, or freeze for up to 1 month.

Light Chicken Stock

3 to 5 pounds chicken bones, including feet and some meatier bones if possible

2 carrots, peeled and chopped

2 to 3 stalks celery, chopped

$1/2$ head garlic, loose skin removed and cloves cracked

1 large onion, chopped

2 whole cloves, stuck into 2 of the onion pieces

3 bay leaves

$1/4$ bunch flat-leaf parsley, stems only

3 or 4 sprigs thyme

1 tablespoon black peppercorns

Remove as much visible fat from the bones as possible. Place the bones in a stockpot and add cold water to cover. Bring to a full rolling boil, skimming off any foam as it rises to the surface. Add all the remaining ingredients and reduce the heat. Simmer, uncovered, skimming as needed, for 3 hours. Strain through a fine-mesh sieve and reduce further, if desired, for storage. Refrigerate until ready to use, or freeze for up to 1 month.

Mushroom Stock

MAKES ABOUT
1 1/2 QUARTS

2 to 3 tablespoons unsalted butter

1 onion, diced

1/2 head garlic, loose skin removed and cloves cracked

2 or 3 carrots, peeled and diced

1 or 2 parsnips, peeled and diced (optional)

2 pounds fresh wild or cultivated mushrooms and trimmings, carefully cleaned

1 ounce dried wild mushrooms

6 to 8 sprigs thyme

6 to 8 flat-leaf parsley stems

1 1/2 teaspoons black peppercorns

Melt the butter in a stockpot over medium-low heat. Add the onion, garlic, carrots, and parsnips and cook over low heat, stirring often, for 8 to 10 minutes, until soft but not brown. Add the mushrooms and cook, stirring, for 1 to 2 minutes more. Add the thyme, parsley, and cold water to cover. Increase the heat to medium-high and bring to a boil, skimming off any impurities that rise to the surface. Reduce the heat to medium-low, add the peppercorns, and simmer, skimming frequently, for 1 hour. Taste and simmer for an additional 30 minutes or so, until reduced and flavorful. Strain through a fine-mesh sieve and refrigerate until ready to use, or freeze for up to 1 month.

Index